Is It Right to Fight?

A FIRST LOOK AT CONFLICT

PAT THOMAS
ILLUSTRATED BY LESLEY HARKER

HODDER
Wayland

an imprint of Hodder Children's Books

Have you ever been so mad that you wanted to yell or scream or even hit someone?

Maybe someone said something mean to you
or broke one of your favourite toys. Perhaps you
got blamed for something you did not do.

Everyone feels angry sometimes. It is OK to feel angry.

Sometimes it is even a good thing, because when
you are treated unfairly anger can give you
the courage to speak out.

But hitting and screaming is never helpful.
It always makes things worse.

What about you?

Have you ever had a fight or argument with
someone? What did you fight about?
Did fighting solve the problem?

Sometimes it is fun to have a play fight.

It can also be fun to play games or watch programmes where people fight but do not get hurt.

But real fighting is
never that much fun.

Fighting can make you so upset that your head and stomach start to hurt.

It can make it hard to sleep or sit still.

If you hit someone or hurt their feelings it can make you feel sad and ashamed.

People fight for lots of different reasons. They fight when they are feeling angry, or scared, or hurt and left out.

Some people fight because they think it makes them look big and strong.

Being around people who are always fighting
can make you feel very unhappy.

Sometimes a friend might ask you to help them fight with others. Other times someone may pick a fight with you for no reason you can understand.

When this happens you may end up fighting
even if you do not really want to.

What about you?

Has this ever happened to you? Can you
think of some ways to avoid fighting?

When you watch television you may hear stories and see pictures of people fighting wars in other parts of the world.

A war is a violent argument between different groups of people.

Many people die because of war every year.

There is hardly ever a good reason to fight.

And although sometimes adults think that they fight for different or better reasons than children, often this is not true.

We can all make our homes and classrooms and
communities more peaceful by remembering
a few simple rules.

Almost any fight can be avoided by learning to take turns, not calling names, not pushing somebody around just because you are bigger than them and apologizing when you are wrong.

It is also important to listen to other people's opinions — even if they are different from yours. Make sure other people listen to your opinions too.

Sometimes it is helpful to have a grown-up, or someone else who will not take sides, to listen.

Once everyone has had their say
then you can begin to think
of different ways to solve the
problem together
peacefully.

Like so many things people do, learning to solve differences without fighting takes practice.

But if we all keep practising, we really can make the world a more peaceful place.

HOW TO USE THIS BOOK

Like all of life's tough lessons, learning how to resolve conflicts peacefully is an ongoing process. Many adults struggle with this idea and children, because of their limited experience of the world, need patience and strong support as they explore better ways of resolving their differences. Before talking with your child about conflict consider these thoughts:

Peaceful conflict resolution takes practice, just like learning to swim or practising the piano. Be patient.

Children learn to resolve conflicts by watching others – especially adults. Fights between parents or other adults, and the way that parents react to children's fights, set the example. So take some time to think about how you resolve conflicts in your own life. If your tendency is to fight or be aggressive, you can hardly blame your children for reacting in the same way.

Teach your children that it is OK to get angry. But also teach them that there are both acceptable and unacceptable ways to express anger. Help your child to know that peacefulness is more than just avoiding anger and violence. Explain that it doesn't mean that people never lose their tempers or act impulsively. It means that people know how to talk to each other, appreciate each other's differences and have a basic willingness to co-operate and compromise.

Let children discuss how they feel about fighting that they see on the television and in the newspapers. Answer their questions as honestly as you can and try to bring world and local news stories down to a level that children can understand. Sadly, most wars are fought for exactly the same reasons that children fight in the playground.

In larger classes it can be hard for teachers to find the time to help children resolve conflicts. Punishment and separating those involved often takes the place of talking things through. However, school is a major source of role models for children and whatever a teacher can do to help promote a dialogue between children is important.

Teachers can help by making children aware of the level of peacefulness in the classroom. You can talk about fighting in weekly discussions, and link it into specific topics (e.g. ancient civilizations such as the Romans or the Victorians).

Try making a 'peace thermometer' with sunny skies and no clouds for a peaceful, co-operative day; clouds and wind indicating a day where people are using angry words and insults; storms for hitting and shoving; and hurricanes indicating major conflicts in class. String a bead through a long piece of string and tape each end to the thermometer. Slide the bead up and down depending on how things are going in the class. Give rewards, such as stickers, for peaceful days. If things are going badly, let the children make suggestions about how to bring the blue skies back.

GLOSSARY

aggression Fierce or threatening behaviour.

ashamed To feel embarrassed or bad about something you have done.

community/communities A group of people who live or work in the same area.

opinion The ideas and beliefs that a person has about something, usually based on their own experience of life.

solve To find the answer to a problem.

BOOKS TO READ

Fiction

Peace Tales
by Margaret Read MacDonald
(Shoe String Press, 1992)

The Seeds of Peace
by Laura Berkley and Alison Dexter
(Barefoot Books, 1999)

The Story of Ferdinand
by Munro Leaf (Puffin, 1988)

Why Are You Fighting, Davy?
by Brigitte Weninger
(North-South Books, 1999)

Non-Fiction

Peace Begins With Me
by Jill Bennett and Peter Bailey
(Oxford University Press, 2001)

Somewhere Today: A Book of Peace
by Shelley Moore Thomas and Eric Futran
(Albert Whitman & Co, 2002)

Why Fight?
by Janine Amos and Annabel Spencely
(Cheery Tree Books, 2000)

For Parent and Adults

Raising a Thinking Child: Help Your Child to Resolve Everyday Conflicts and Get Along With Others
by Myrna B Shure and Theresa Foy Digeronimo
(Pocket Books, 1996)